DON'T PLAGUE

AND

FORTY YEARS OF IRISH FERRIES

BY

TREVOR BOULT

Published by
STRANRAER AND DISTRICT LOCAL HISTORY TRUST

This book is dedicated to the officers and crews of the *Stena Galloway* and *Stena Caledonia*, and the shore support staff at Stranraer and Belfast.

ISBN   0 9535776 6 X

Published by
Stranraer and District Local History Trust
Tall Trees
London Road
Stranraer DG9 8BZ

DON'T PLAGUE THE FERRYMAN

AND

FORTY YEARS OF IRISH FERRIES

Introduction

The symbolic maritime link between Stranraer and Tyneside is strong. It is a poignant coincidence that perhaps the most significant ship ever to have sailed from Stranraer now resides opposite the grand Newcastle waterfront, beneath the famous 'coathanger' arch of the Tyne Bridge.

Known and loved by countless travellers of the traditional short sea route to Northern Ireland, the Caledonian Princess brings latter-day pleasures of a different kind to Tyneside revellers. To those who know her glorious past, it may seem ignominious that the Tuxedo Princess is a floating nightclub. Yet this particular Geordie can easily turn back the clock several decades and recall the thrill of a young boy standing above the stern, as the 'Princess' left the railway pier at Stranraer, bound for Larne and its promise of summer holidays at the family farm in Antrim. The ship continued to speak to me down the years. As a Merchant Navy navigating officer, I eventually seized my chance to work on a later generation of Princess.

Launched as the Galloway Princess and known today as the Stena Galloway, she is the eldest of the current fleet of conventional ferries and has forged an appreciative following of her own.

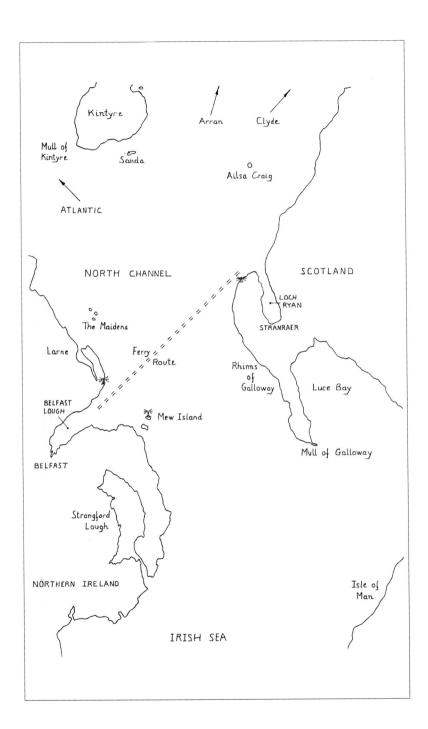

DON'T PLAGUE THE FERRYMAN

An uneasy union takes place at Gretna Green. Here, the road sign boasts that Stranraer is 100 miles away. It is a far outreach to be confronted by the raw material of work as a ro-ro ferry's loading and navigating officer. Yet the sinewy tentacle is unmistakable. On the one linking trunk-road west from the M6, the convoys of heavy articulated lorries hurtle insistently to and from the Loch Ryan ports, and their promise of Northern Ireland.

With the unlooked-for zeal of a train-spotter, mere glimpses of distant lorry liveries are confirmed as regular shippers: Dukes; Woodside Haulage; Montgomery's; McBurney Bros.; Irving Transport; to name but a few. They come with a mental set of dimensions, weights, problems of stowage and the dull smart of wounds from the many hard lessons learned in the harsh arena of a ship's vehicle decks.

As I continue to discover, there is a lot more to quickly and safely loading a stately twin-deck ro-ro ferry with anything from 100-tonne heavy lifts to motorcycles, on an exposed short-sea route. It had seemed effortless — as an observer....

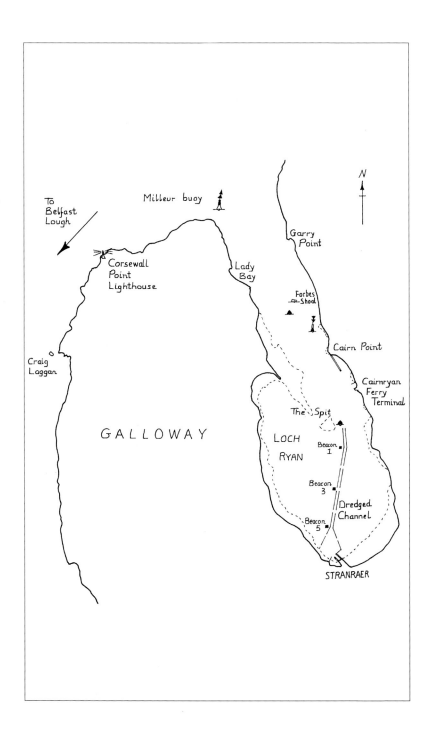

To
Belfast
Lough

Milleur buoy

Corsewall
Point
Lighthouse

Garry
Point

Lady
Bay

Forbes
Shoal

Cairn Point

Craig
Laggan

Cairnryan
Ferry
Terminal

GALLOWAY

The Spit

LOCH
RYAN

Beacon
1

Beacon
3

Dredged
Channel

Beacon
5

STRANRAER

N

THE STENA GALLOWAY

'Galloway fore and aft; let go!' The radioed acknowledgments echoed loudly on the lofty starboard bridge-wing, as the awaiting crews at their stations were galvanised into action. To the whir of winches, the remaining taut ropes were slackened, and cast off ashore.

'Gone and clear aft; clear channel astern,' came the advice from the officer on the poop, braced against a northerly chill. As the night-captain leaned on the pair of heavy pitch-control levers, and delicately adjusted the bow thruster, the Stena Galloway eased off her berth at Stranraer. 'Lower the visor', was the order sent to the cargoman at his blind controls on the main deck. Slowly the raised section of bow descended as the ship gathered sternway.

It is 2.30 a.m. on a midweek autumn night. In the neoned gloom beyond the retreating Ross Pier a pair of herons, with necks stretched and haughty poise, stalk the low-tide shallows. Most of Stranraer is sleeping, indifferent to the nocturnal activity at the port which sustains it. With a substantial cargo of mixed heavy freight and light passenger traffic, Stena Galloway — grand old lady of the current fleet — maintains the historic connection to Northern Ireland with her sister the Stena Caledonia, and the high-speed Stena Voyager.

'Green light on the visor', is reported back to the cargoman below, as the bridge indicator-panel shows the bow is secure. Beyond the chevron of the heavy bow doors, a crewman descends the vertical ladder to inspect visually the securing cleats. This final check reported to the bridge, the business of tightly turning the ship focuses the captain's attention. With a subtly-defined manoeuvring area, it requires a canny local knowledge to ensure the swinging stern does not fall foul of the unforgiving shallows.

'Provided I keep in line with the railway pier, and I don't exceed the transit between my house and the life-boat shed, I know the stern will stay inside the swinging area', intimated the captain. It was one of many references not to be found in any manual of navigation. Yet it brought added certainty to complement the official beacons, in the hard-won experience from thousands of such manoeuvres.

Take her inside please, helmsman; steer for the Cairn light,' was the next order. With a clunk of switches, the steering and propulsion controls revert to the bridge. Beyond the windows and

Stena Galloway at Stranraer.
Photo: Trevor Boult.

Main vehicle deck of the Galloway showing the internal ramps of the upper deck above.
Photo: Trevor Boult.

their sweeping wipers, the bright green flashing light of No. 5 beacon lies fine on the port bow; the first of four marks defining the two-mile dredged channel leading towards the ferry terminal of Cairnryan.

Gladly quitting the open poop deck with its heavily-lashed cargo of hazardous goods, the loading officer inspects both vehicle decks before climbing the many stairs to the bridge. Out of breath, but otherwise satisfied, he reports 'All secure below'.

Rounding the Scar buoy that marks the southern extremity of the Spit bank, the shore lights of the little township of Cairnryan command the forward view. Lurking unseen in between lies the lengthy unlit finger of Cairnryan jetty. Once resounding to the clamour of the breakers' yard, and the earlier glory of a naval base, it is now largely redundant. Its lurking inky blackness is a hazard not to be overlooked. Ferries are careful to line up at a cable's distance when passing the adjacent Cairn Point light, the stocky lighthouse with its flashing red signal. Here is a tight constriction of navigable water, before the channel gently widens towards the green and red flashing buoys at the Forbes Shoal, a mile beyond. At anchor off nearby Lady Bay, a Northern Lighthouse Board tender awaits daylight, to attend the annual maintenance of these marks.

To benefit as yet unseen approaching ferries, an announcement over the VHF warns of the ship's position, and her imminent exit from the all-concealing loch. 'Full-away' is rung to the engine-room and as the bows begin to gently lift and dip to the rumour of the open sea, the watchkeeper may enjoy the unfolding drama. Ahead, the regular white flash of the Milleur buoy marks the turning point and mouth of Loch Ryan. As it comes abeam, a ghostly loom of light sculpts a black and rocky bluff. The next moment, the ship is raked by the full beam of Corsewall Point lighthouse. The rain on the windows sparkles, briefly throwing the helmsman's profile into statuesque relief.

As the helm is put gently to port, searching eyes scan westwards for immediate signs of expected in-bound traffic, and for any other shipping. It can be as spectacular an entry into congested waters as from any South Coast port.

The ship heels gently to the insistent force of the strong north-westerly wind; the short sea jostles the bow. Allowing a generous sea-room off the lee shore of Corsewall, the pair of fin stabilisers are extended as a matter of course in such weather. As they begin their steadying influence, the indicator needles move silently on the bridge gauges. In the engine control-room, the droning hydraulics become just one more sound for the watchkeepers to absorb.

As the lighthouse bears south, a south-westerly course is set towards distant Belfast Lough; a practised allowance made for the combined effects of wind and a burgeoning flood tide. On the radar screen, detected targets are plotted. Ahead, the corresponding faint pinheads of lights confirm the visibility. The lights grow and gel into familiar arrangements. On the port bow, the Stena Caledonia; to starboard the overhauling Stena Voyager. In short minutes all three vessels are in transit. It offers an indulgent moment to see one's self, in passing. Soon, the VHF announces: 'Fast craft information, Stena Voyager off Corsewall Point, in-bound for Loch Ryan.'

The tracks of conventional and fast P&O ferries on the route from Larne paint their familiar trails on the radar. A selection of other more-random moving targets represents the unknown. All are monitored carefully; appraising binoculars are raised in scrutiny. Here, the 20-mile wide North Channel can be busy with through traffic, fishing vessels and seasonal yachts. The mouth of Belfast Lough, defined by the lighthouses of Black Head and Mew Island, sees the passage of many commercial vessels using its port facilities. In-bound from Liverpool, the Mersey Viking rounds Mew Island and makes for the long white flash of the Fairway buoy. On schedule, she reports to the harbour radio 20 minutes ahead of the Galloway.

In the lee of the Antrim coast, the stabilisers are retracted. On her own approach into the neon-rimmed expanse of the lough, the risks of forgetful familiarity are amply guarded against; the sequence of many small but vital tasks are ticked off on the Belfast arrival checklist: shaft alternator off; clear anchors; ring stand-by; advise harbour at No. 14 beacon; request hydraulics and exhaust fans; fire alarms to in-port mode....

Thrusting three-quarters of a mile out from the northern shore of Belfast Lough, the unlit length of Cloghan jetty is guarded by the off-lying Cloghan buoy, with its quick-flashing green light. As it is passed, binoculars are directed towards the shorter but better-lit Kilroot jetty. At its exposed extremity a small freighter is seen which would be vulnerable to the effects of a passing ship's wake and out of courtesy the Galloway gives more sea-room.

Reverting to hand steering, the ship sweeps a gentle arc towards the Fairway buoy, outlier to the channel into Belfast and the start of pilotage waters. Holding pilotage exemption for the

10

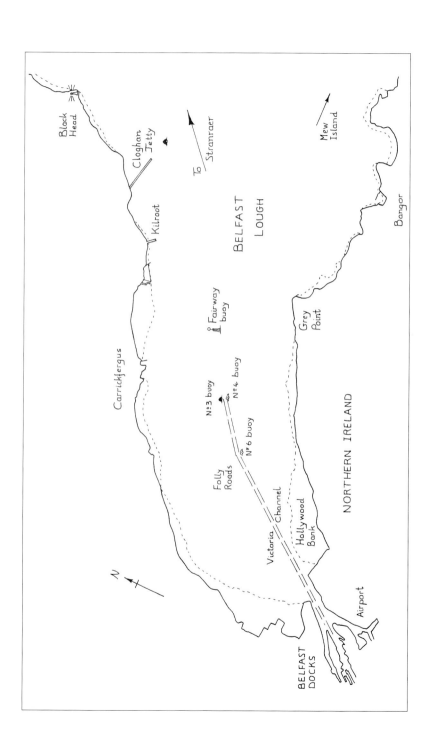

port, the attending captain quietly monitors the watch officer's actions. The process of in-house training is thorough and on-going; a proven formula to nurture experience with imparted advice across the broad range of conditions of weather and traffic movements.

Passing swiftly between the first pair of buoys, a gentle dog-leg brings the ship's head towards the green and red flashes of the markers at the disturbingly-named Folly Roads. The strong beam wind off the hills beyond Carrickfergus heels the ship like a well reefed schooner. Like any true ship-under-sail, the course of the Galloway is adjusted to compensate for a considerable leeway. Bells ring loudly on the bridge; the indicator buttons flash yellow as they are pushed for the order 'Stand-by engines'.

As the series of red flashing beacons that mark the east side of the three-mile dredged channel come into line, the helm order 'Steer 219' is given. On both sides, the well-spaced and staggered beacon lights flash incessantly, each with a different character. Heading crabwise up the channel that appears all too narrow in such conditions, in the distance the bulk of the Mersey Viking seems to fill the turning basin as she also engages the wind that blows strongly off her berth.

Slowly passing the tanker Anchorman, berthed at the refinery jetty, and the container ships at the busy Victoria Terminal, the Mersey Viking has completed her swing and is sending ropes ashore. Passing the narrows between the East and West twin beacons, the Galloway prepares to make her own careful swing to port, in the confines next to Thompson Dock.

'Swinging clear aft,' reports the officer on the poop, as the heavy stern-gates rattle excitedly above the turmoil of the contrary-thrusting propellers. With a feigned disinterest, the close manoeuvre entertains a crew nightwatchman on the big bulk carrier working cargo at the grain berth. 'Clear channel' is reported, as the ship begins her half-mile passage stern first to the ro-ro berth. Reporting marks keeps the captain on the bridge-wing informed, as finally the stern is canted towards the double tier of raised ramps. To the captain's order, across the public address system, passengers are requested to proceed to their vehicles. The announcement echoes loudly off the terminal buildings. Urged by his father at their high vantage point, with great reluctance a small boy peels his fingers off the rails, denied the final spectacle of docking.

Heaving lines are thrown and the winches whir again. Peering intently overside, the critical countdown is relayed to the bridge: '15-feet; 10; 5...' As the white guide marks on ship and quay coincide, the controlling rope is deftly secured on the bitts to prevent further movement. Linesmen haul the long bow and stern ropes to their bollards. All fast, and 'Finished with engines', the controllable-pitch propellers cease their turning. A momentary peace descends on the poop.

Elsewhere throughout the ship, the various departments switch to in-port routine; within the hour the Galloway is scheduled to sail. Hotel staff efficiently clean the homely and well-appointed public spaces. Brass pillars and mirrored surfaces are polished; beneath gallery paintings the table-top oil cloths gleam; the plush carpet pile knows the gentle scuff of a vacuum cleaner as much as the tread of passengers. The cook prepares the next round of meals, to the accompaniment of his own brand of taped music. On the quayside, the black BP road tanker, with its delivery of fuel oil, awaits the opening of the ship's low bunker door. On the poop deck high above, the fresh water hose fizzles contentedly as it too replenishes.

Soon its sound is lost in the cacophony of discharging the vehicle decks. As the huge hydraulic doors on the twin decks open, and the fingers of the lowering ramps emphatically meet the steel decks, the roar of many lorry engines adds to that of the ventilation fans, to reverberate within the enclosed sounding-box of the upper deck. With a directing wave from the hard-hatted, day-glow-dressed cargoman, lit like a stage performer by the rank of headlights, the

Sending the sternline ashore at Belfast.
Photo: Trevor Boult.

13

View from the bridge of the Stena Galloway as she passes the Stena Voyager.
Photo: Trevor Boult.

ponderous convoy is teased out into a straggly line. Each articulated lorry vies with its neighbour to be off sooner and once more on the road.

The main deck beneath disgorges similar 'running' traffic, leaving behind lorries with no drivers and trailers with no cabs. These are discharged by the shore team who remove the 'unaccompanied' vehicles to the lorry park, and adroitly tow off the tightly stowed lines of trailers with tractor-tugs. Clear of all traffic, the ship's loading officer begins to determine and direct the sequence for back-loading the already waiting cargo.

Now lightened, and on a rising tide, the moorings are eased; the ship must not be 'hanging on the ropes' when judging the disposition of the incoming load, to sail with the ship upright.

'We have about 40 cars — the occupant of one requiring use of the lift — 18 trailers and a dozen artics at the moment, eels for the poop and some livestock — sheep; is it okay to carry them?' queries the team leader ashore. Confirmed, loading begins apace, working both decks simultaneously. The four man crew on each deck labour at guiding and chaining each delivery of trailers, as varied as milk tankers, refrigerated units, acid boxes, Parcel Force wagons and lengthy girder-bearing flat-beds.

The car for the lift is given special treatment, its occupants being escorted by hotel staff from the din of the main deck into the calm of the lounges. The cars 'pair up' across the lanes on the upper deck, leaving ample space for late traffic, small or heavy. Ever mindful of the maxim 'Always load for a potential full load', every earning space is well considered. As the draught gauges indicate the ever-changing trim and list of the ship throughout loading, the game of 3-D chess is played out by the loading officer, to complete loading with proper stability. The elusive 'upright' condition haunts the mind.

'Send in the artics, light going heavy please...' requests the officer to shore, '...I need some stern trim: make the livestock No. 7.' The three-tiered carrier of the rain-damp sheep is guided to the flat mid-section of the main deck and well chained. Supply and exhaust fans to the area are requested from the engine-room. The internal upper deck load completed, the lorry with its tanks of eels is directed onto the poop. The ship's fire main is connected to supply a trickle of salt water into the tanks with their unseen yet seething cargo.

'Belfast Harbour, Stena Galloway; ready to sail in 20 minutes' is relayed from the bridge, as the steering and propulsion systems are tested. At the stability computer, loading figures are being entered, awaiting the final details from the main deck.

Launch of Galloway Princess, Harland & Wolff, Belfast.
Photo: Captain D. J. Ramsey.

The Galloway Princess in original Sealink livery.
Photo: Donnie Nelson.

New owners, new name: Stena Galloway.
Photo: Donnie Nelson.

'Main deck to bridge; ramp on the move; 746 tonnes; one car; passenger figure 137.' A subtle relief is heard in the officer's voice. It is a pleasant indulgence to stand, rain-oblivious, on the poop deck for letting go, and look upwards beyond the sternlight to the mast and know that the perverse gremlins to the 'upright condition' have not held sway.

From her upstream terminal on the River Lagan, Seacat Scotland has left her berth and is passing the Galloway. Looming above her sleek twin-hulled form, at Queens Wharf the huge historic letters HARLAND & WOLFF pronounce shipbuilding glories of the past; not least the four sister ships of which the Stena Galloway is the eldest.

On the bridge-wing, the day-captain is resigned to the almost obligatory deluge of rain that mischievously accompanies many dock manoeuvres. He accepts it with almost boyish delight, brushing the beads of water off the pitch gauges and gripping the burnished brass rudder control. Ahead, the HSS Stena Voyager is backing onto the link-span. As docking cleats engage in her transom, she becomes 'All fast'. Gone is the need for her to use mooring ropes. As the Galloway passes close down the side of the Voyager, from the glasshouse of her elevated and enclosed bridge, a small torch waves a disembodied greeting to those lucky enough to have a bridge-wing — and the feel

'Swinging clear aft': The Galloway turning in Belfast Harbour, prior to docking stern first.
Photo: Trevor Boult.

'The fingers of the shore ramp emphatically meet the deck'.
Photo: Trevor Boult.

of rain. Also braving the elements, observing passengers lean hunch-shouldered at the boat deck rails.

Leaving the port of Belfast, the lights of the channel beacons show more clearly against the less cluttered illumination from shore. The landing lights of aircraft on their final approach to the harbourside airport reflect brightly off the shallow waters of Hollywood Bank, already gouged into a rhythmic pattern of waves by the passing of the ship.

'Stena Galloway — pass beacon No. 10 slowly please; a crane-barge is working there', advises Harbour Radio. As the ship finally clears the channel and heads towards the first glimmer of dawn, the 12-hour nightshift comes off duty for grateful rest.

With limited sleeping accommodation for passengers, tired drivers still find comfortable spots to sleep, stretched out and switched off; unlike the Flying Dutchman wakefulness of the gaming machines that endlessly run their screen diversions of car rallies and martial art combats, clocking up unacknowledged scores in the passing of time.

In the friendly fantasy world of the children's playroom, the rainbow colours of the bouncy mats, together with the murals of Winnie the Pooh and Tom and Jerry, inspire its young occupants to loll or leap with safe abandon. In the adjacent video lounge, relaxing parents join with other viewers to become absorbed in an all-action movie, oblivious to the real-life spectacle taking place at the other end of the ship.

A Wessex military helicopter exercises with the Stena Galloway.
Photo: Trevor Boult.

Hovering with uncanny perfection in the much abated wind, the dark shape of a Wessex military helicopter fills the bridge windows. The jarring vibration of its thrashing rotors denies speech. The row of gathered faces mutely spectate, as the Galloway holds her course and speed. Carrying out a routine exercise, the airman is winched to the bow visor's meagre-sized deck. Radioed thanks accompany the helicopter's receding form, as quiet returns. On the southward horizon, the tiny pale silhouettes of naval ships silently move to the rigours of their own exercises.

Left in peace for the remainder of the one-hour channel crossing, the watchkeeper and lookout may indulge in the crisp clarity of the morning air. The Mull of Kintyre and the mountains of Arran adorn the distant northern view; the lengthy hammerhead of the Rhinns of Galloway fill the horizon on the starboard bow. To port, the remote cloud-capped splendour of Ailsa Craig displays its hayrick aspect. Outward from its own high cliffs, a group of brilliant-white gannets wings its purposeful way low beyond the Galloway's bows. Outward from the Clyde, a well-laden coaster pursues her own southerly course.

At the helm controls on the Stena Galloway, minor adjustments are made to her course, to pass Corsewall Point lighthouse at an appropriate distance. Not only a functioning lighthouse and a Grade 'A' listed building of national importance, it is also a unique luxury hotel and restaurant. Perchance that from its windows a guest may be watching the progress of the passing shipping.

As the Galloway reverts once more to hand steering, before the entrance to Loch Ryan, an outward P&O ferry rounds the Milleur buoy at speed. Several minutes later, the Galloway also adds her wake as she sweeps into the head of the loch. Responding to the shallower confines, the wake gradually evolves into a pursuing parade of steep standing waves. With an expectant eye on the flashing numbers of the echo-sounder, at 5 metres 'Stand-by engines' is rung, on nearing the Forbes Shoal. As the propulsion is eased, the ship's stern rises perceptibly; with drag reduced she continues her way with renewed grace and economy.

In the chartroom corner, the kettle boils for the relief watchkeeper's first cup of the day. Opposite, a display of red electronic digits cleverly indicates the wind speed and direction in the harbour, and the height of tide at the approaching No. 1 beacon. About its green conical structure, cormorants, with drying wings timelessly outstretched, share the platform with the solar panel's smooth technology. They ignore the familiar passing ship that rears above them.

Stena Voyager passing the Cairn light.
Photo: Donnie Nelson.

'Down the channel please, helmsman', the captain orders, as the speed is further adjusted to reach the turning circle as the Stena Voyager departs her berth on time.

Arrival preparations complete and reported from all departments, the Galloway's bows are pointed in turn at the locally-known marks: 'Captain Bob's house; Town Pier; end of the Ross; middle bus-stop...' As control once more transfers to the bridge-wing, the bright sunshine of docking reflects a buoyant mood; it is crew change-over day; the week's duty is nearly done.

The raised bow visor's holding hooks slip quietly into place; the ship and shore buffers gently meet. 'All fast for'd',... 'All fast aft'....

Like any other seafarer the world over, when leaving ship the ferryman casts a final scan around the cabin that was home away from home. The eye glimpses the small painting on the bulkhead of the Clyde puffer Vital Spark, stoutly confronting the chops of the channel under a leaden sky. Ashore, in the nearby Waterloo Art Gallery, hangs a fine pastel of the Stena Galloway. Resplendent in her present livery, it is a local celebration as fitting as the model on permanent display in the National Maritime Museum, in her original colours as the Galloway Princess.

With a fresh crew, the Stena Galloway once more departs Stranraer on her noon sailing, bathed in the sunlight of a crisp autumn day. Yet in the water-front Agnew Park, an anchor-topped hewn granite memorial carries a plaque bearing a poignant message. It is a reminder of unchanging perils, and of the unsung vigilance that accompanies a ferry departing for the open sea. It reads:

'On the morning of January 31st 1953, MV Princess Victoria left Stranraer for Larne on a normal crossing, and met a gale that caused so much damage and loss of life throughout the country. The vessel foundered off the coast of Northern Ireland. 133 were lost. 23 were inhabitants of Stranraer.'

By the clocktower, the red ensign flies proudly; in quiet praise of the ferryman.

The Caledonian Princess, complete with its Lion Rampant on the funnel in Loch Ryan in 1964.

Photo: Donnie Nelson.

New livery, new name: the Tuxedo Princess on the Tyne as a floating nightclub, 1998.

Photo: Trevor Boult.

THE 'CALEY P' AND FORTY YEARS

The Caledonian Princess — affectionately known to many as the Caley P — proved to be the modern saviour of the North Channel route from Stranraer. In the first two years of operation, she far exceeded the challenge presented by the British Transport Commission, to single-handedly turn previous losses into profit.

Under a dedicated management by the Caledonian Steam Packet Company (Irish Services) Ltd., the Caledonian Princess successfully competed against airlines, and was to treat with disdain the loss of the direct rail link from Dumfries, in the Beeching closures. A huge increase in traffic was generated and the long-term viability of the route was secured.

An innovative vessel for her time, the Clyde-built passenger car-ferry exhibited high quality craftsmanship, decoration and levels of comfort in her cabins and public spaces. Substantially larger than earlier vessels and with turbine propulsion that gave her an impressive speed in excess of twenty knots, she was enthusiastically received. Prior to her inaugural sailing from Stranraer to Larne in December 1961, the ship was the focus of an eagerly-anticipated open day at both ports.

Integrating with train services, the Caledonian Princess soon became established on her schedule of two round-trips per day. Resplendent in fine livery and exuberant yellow funnel, adorned with the red lion rampant, she was to grace Loch Ryan and Larne for a decade, before leaving the North Channel route. The Caledonian Princess and the spirit of travel she engendered is recalled and celebrated to this day, in the classic and colourful poster displayed in the foyer of the Sea Terminal at Stranraer.

The success of the route justified the building of a second new ship. In December 1967, the equally innovative Antrim Princess came into service. To cope with demand in the interim, the Stena Nordica joined the route early in 1966. She was the first representative of a different company and a glimpse well into the future, when Stena Line would become the main operator out of Stranraer.

The first purpose-built drive-through ferry for the route, the Antrim Princess eventually took over from the Caley P as principal ship, releasing her for winter relief work elsewhere in the Irish Sea. In April 1972, the Caledonian Princess returned to Stranraer to bid farewell to her home port, before relocating to Fishguard, in South

Wales. The North Channel route was then served by the Antrim Princess and the similar Ailsa Princess, which came into service in the summer of 1971. The service was to be additionally supported by a succession of chartered freight ships.

In 1973, a new port facility at Cairnryan opened up competition. Several ferry companies have operated from there, P&O being the latest to take advantage of the shorter crossing time. In 1978, the ferry-handling facilities at Stranraer and Larne were enhanced by the introduction of two-tier link-spans. These were to herald a new era; of larger vessels with double decks, able to load and discharge quickly, both decks being worked at the same time.

In May 1980, the new purpose-built ferry Galloway Princess entered service on the North Channel route. Built for Sealink by Harland and Wolff, the distinctive twin-funnelled vessel was capable of carrying 1000 passengers and up to 300 cars. Internal moveable ramps which linked main and upper-deck enhanced her flexibility of operation. The Antrim Princess was freed for service elsewhere, but periodically revisited the route to cover during overhauls.

In the summer of 1984, Sealink UK Ltd. was sold into the private sector. In 1986, the Galloway Princess was to share the route with a sister ship, the former Sealink cross-channel ferry, St. David.

1990 saw Sealink being taken over by Stena Line. The following year, the St. Christopher, another sister ship from the English Channel, joined the route. Their names were changed: Galloway Princess became Stena Galloway; St. David became Stena Caledonia. The newcomer was renamed Stena Antrim. All three bore the new hull-side logo Stena Sealink.

In the summer of 1992, SeaCat Scotland created a terminal at Stranraer. They introduced a fast ferry link to Northern Ireland, becoming until recently an effective competitor to the established operators in Loch Ryan. Towards the end of 1995, Stena transferred their route to Belfast. This brought to a close an era of over 120 years service between Stranraer and Larne.

1996 was to see the ships bearing the logo Stena Line. In the summer, the route welcomed yet another generation of innovative vessel, the HSS Stena Voyager. Served by dedicated link-spans and enhanced marshalling facilities, the Voyager eventually displaced the Stena Antrim from the route.

The Stena Voyager caters for the many passengers and commercial shippers who require a rapid crossing of the North Channel. As conventional ferries, the Stena Galloway and Stena Caledonia offer an equally essential, if less proclaimed, service. They each provide 32 crossings weekly, on the summer schedule, with a slight reduction over the winter. Substantial loads of heavy freight are shipped, especially on the overnight sailings. At any time, the more leisurely pace and open deck areas foster the more traditional values of sea travel. They display an enviable record of continuing to operate in severe weather, at times accepting traffic from cancelled sailings by other vessels, both locally and from further afield.

In-house training on the Stena Galloway as she leaves the dock at Stranraer.

Photo: Trevor Boult.

The Stena Galloway, departing from Belfast, passes the HSS Stena Discovery.
Photo: Alan Geddes.

Acknowledgment

The author kindly acknowledges the assistance of Captain S. Horne, Senior Master, Stena Galloway, in the preparation of this book.

The book has been published by the Stranraer and District Local History Trust which was constituted in 1998 at the instigation of Stranraer and District Chamber of Commerce. The objectives of this Trust are to research, record and publish information on local history for the benefit of the community.

Previous Trust publications:

Stranraer in World War Two
   — Archie Bell.

The Loss of the Princess Victoria
   — Jack Hunter.

The Cairnryan Military Railway 1941-1959
   — Bill Gill.

A Peep at Stranraer's Past
   — Donnie Nelson.

Royal Burgh of Stranraer 1617-1967-2000
   — John S. Boyd, Jack Hunter, Donnie Nelson,
     Christine L. Wilson.

Membership 2000 - 2001